Pebble Plus

SEA LIFE

SEA STARS

by **Mari Schuh**

Consulting Editor:
Gail Saunders-Smith, PhD

Consultant:
Jody Rake, Member,
Southwest Marine Educators Association

CAPSTONE PRESS
a capstone imprint

Pebble Plus is published by Capstone Press,
1710 Roe Crest Drive, North Mankato, Minnesota 56003
www.capstonepub.com

Library of Congress Cataloging-in-Publication Data
Schuh, Mari C.
Sea stars / by Mari Schuh.
p. cm. — (Pebble plus. Sea Life)
Includes bibliographical references and index.
Summary: "Describes the characteristics, food, habitat, and behavior of sea stars"—Provided by publisher.
Audience: Age 5-7
Audience: K to grade 3.
ISBN 978-1-4914-6044-3 (library binding)
ISBN 978-1-4914-6064-1 (eBook PDF)
1. Starfishes—Juvenile literature. I. Title.
QL384.A8S38 2016
593.9'3—dc23

Editorial Credits
Elizabeth R. Johnson, editor; Aruna Rangarajan, designer;
Kelly Garvin, media researcher; Tori Abraham, production specialist

Photo Credits
Newscom/Gordon MacSkimming/PictureNature/Photoshot, 19; SeaPics.com: Andrew J. Martinez, 17, Celeste Fowler, 11, Doug Perrine, 15, Tim Hellier, 21; Shutterstock: Andrea Izzotti, cover, 9, 13, Godruma, cover (background), Longjourneys, 7, Vilainecrevette, 5

Design Elements: Shutterstock: Kasia, SusIO, Vectomart

Note to Parents and Teachers

The Sea Life set supports national science standards related to life science. This book describes and illustrates sea stars. The images support early readers in understanding the text. The repetition of words and phrases helps early readers learn new words. This book also introduces early readers to subject-specific vocabulary words, which are defined in the Glossary section. Early readers may need assistance to read some words and to use the Table of Contents, Glossary, Read More, Internet Sites, and Index sections of the book.

Printed in China by Nordica
0415/CA21500542
032015   008837NORDF15

Table of Contents

Life in the Ocean

Sea stars crawl
on the ocean floor.
These colorful animals
look for food to eat.

Sea stars live in oceans around the world. There are about 1,500 kinds of sea stars. They are found in both shallow and deep water.

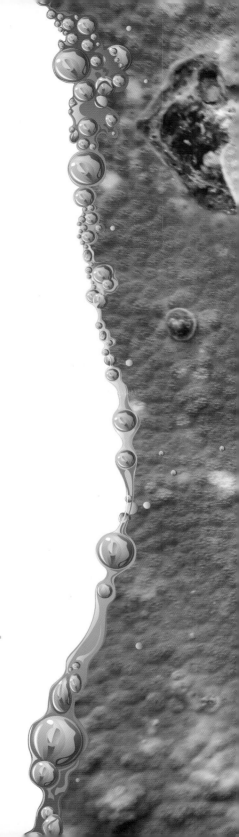

Up Close

Most sea stars have five arms.
Some have 40 arms!
If a sea star loses an arm,
it can grow a new one.

Sea stars can be many sizes.
Some are less than 1 inch
(2.5 centimeters) wide.
Others grow to be more
than 3 feet (1 meter) wide.

Sea stars have tough skin
on their thick arms.
Short spines protect sea
stars from predators.

Sea stars have hundreds
of tiny tube feet.
Their feet help them
crawl on coral reefs
and rocky shores.
Their feet grab prey too.

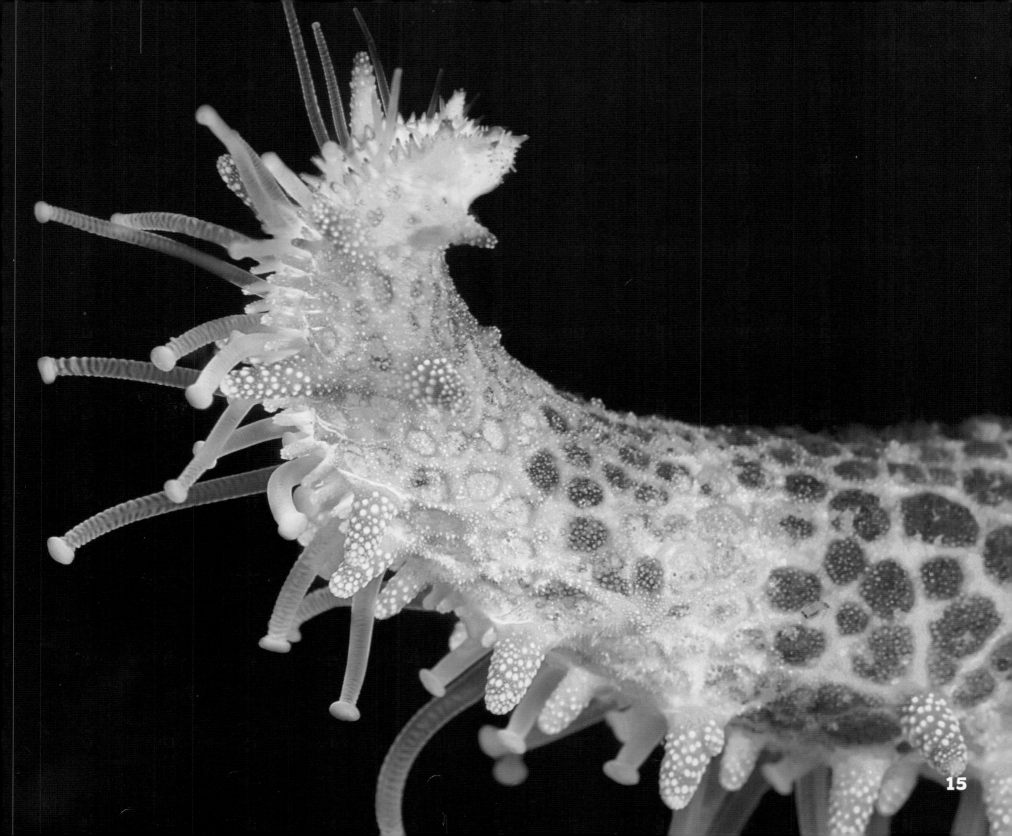

Finding Food

Sea stars open clam shells with their feet. They push their stomachs outside their bodies. They stick their stomachs inside the clam shells. Then sea stars eat their prey.

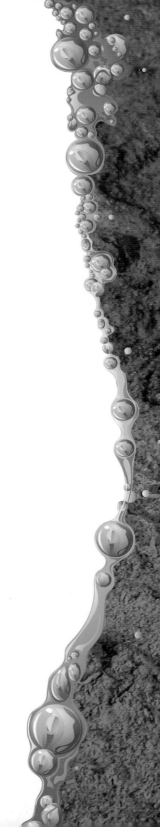

17

Life Cycle

Some female sea stars lay thousands of eggs. Male sea stars put sperm into the water. When the eggs and sperm meet, the eggs are fertilized.

19

The fertilized eggs grow
into tiny larvae.
The larvae float in the
ocean for up to 45 days.
Then they grow into sea
stars on the ocean floor.

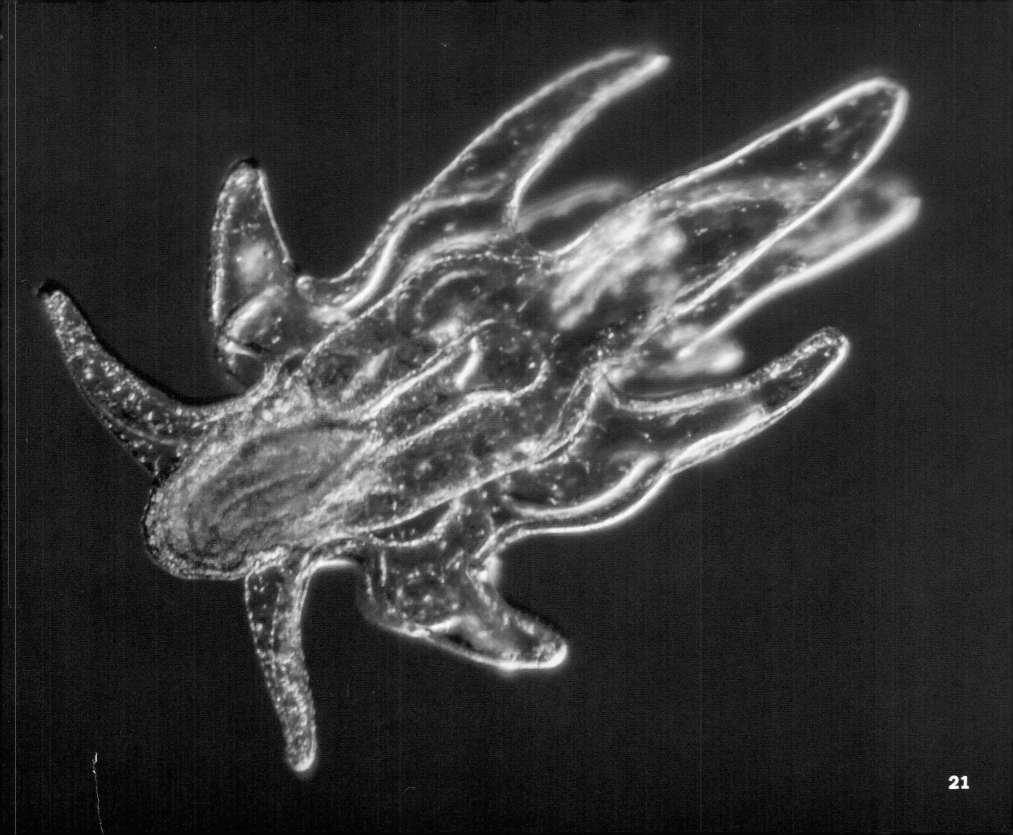

Glossary

coral reef—a type of land close to the surface of the ocean made up of the hardened bodies of corals; corals are small, colorful sea creatures

fertilize—to join an egg of a female with a sperm of a male to produce young

larva—an animal at the stage of development between an egg and an adult; more than one larva are larvae

predator—an animal that hunts other animals for food

prey—an animal hunted by another animal for food

protect—to guard or keep something safe from harm

shallow—not deep

sperm—one of the reproductive cells from a male that is capable of fertilizing eggs in a female

spine—a hard, sharp, pointed growth on an animal's body

Read More

Gibbs, Maddie. *Sea Stars.* Fun Fish. New York: PowerKids Press, 2014.

Hughes, Catherine D. *First Big Book of the Ocean.* National Geographic Little Kids. Washington, D.C.: National Geographic Kids, 2013.

Meister, Cari. *Sea Stars.* Life Under the Sea. Minneapolis: Bullfrog Books, 2013.

Internet Sites

FactHound offers a safe, fun way to find Internet sites related to this book. All of the sites on FactHound have been researched by our staff.

Here's all you do:

Visit *www.facthound.com*

Type in this code: 9781491460443

 Check out projects, games and lots more at **www.capstonekids.com**

Index

Word Count: 212

Grade: 1

Early-Intervention Level: 13